PARENTS
HERE AND THERE

A Kid's Guide to DEPLOYMENT

Marie-Therese Miller

Special thanks to Stephanie Garrity,
Executive Director Rainbows for
All Children

Lerner Publications ◆ Minneapolis

To my husband, John; my dad, Harold; my father-in-law, Warren; and all my family members and friends who bravely served in the US military. With heartfelt thanks to all US armed forces personnel.

Lerner Publications Company
An imprint of Lerner Publishing Group, Inc.
241 First Avenue North
Minneapolis, MN 55401 USA

For reading levels and more information, look up this title at www.lernerbooks.com.

Main body text set in Stempel Garamond Bold.
Typeface provided by Adobe Systems.

Editor: Rebecca Higgins **Designer:** Susan Fienhage

Library of Congress Cataloging-in-Publication Data

Names: Miller, Marie-Therese, author.
Title: Parents here and there : a kid's guide to deployment / Marie-Therese Miller.
Description: Minneapolis : Lerner Publications, [2021] | Includes bibliographical references and index. | Audience: Ages 4–9 | Audience: Grades 2–3 | Summary: "This guide offers an accessible approach to life with a deployed parent and presents helpful information on how to stay in touch. While routines change, the love for a parent doesn't"— Provided by publisher.
Identifiers: LCCN 2020016041 (print) | LCCN 2020016042 (ebook) | ISBN 9781728403434 (library binding) | ISBN 9781728423869 (paperback) | ISBN 9781728418605 (ebook)
Subjects: LCSH: Children of military personnel—United States—Juvenile literature. | Deployment (Strategy)—Psychological aspects—Juvenile literature. | Separation anxiety in children—Juvenile literature. | Families of military personnel—United States—Juvenile literature.
Classification: LCC UB403 .M5373 2021 (print) | LCC UB403 (ebook) | DDC 355.1/2—dc23

LC record available at https://lccn.loc.gov/2020016041
LC ebook record available at https://lccn.loc.gov/2020016042

Manufactured in the United States of America
1-48339-48881-9/17/2020

OurFamilyWizard® is proud to be involved with *Parents Here and There*. We are forever grateful to all those who have served our country, often sacrificing so much to protect the rest of us. When we created OurFamilyWizard®, we immediately saw how military service impacts not only the soldiers but everyone in their lives, especially their families. We hope that this book serves as another show of our appreciation to military service members and creates a practical tool to help children dealing with a variety of emotions when their parent is deployed.

TABLE OF CONTENTS

DEPLOYED PARENTS

All families are special, and parents have all kinds of jobs.

Some work in the military. They keep our country safe.

Sometimes military parents are deployed.

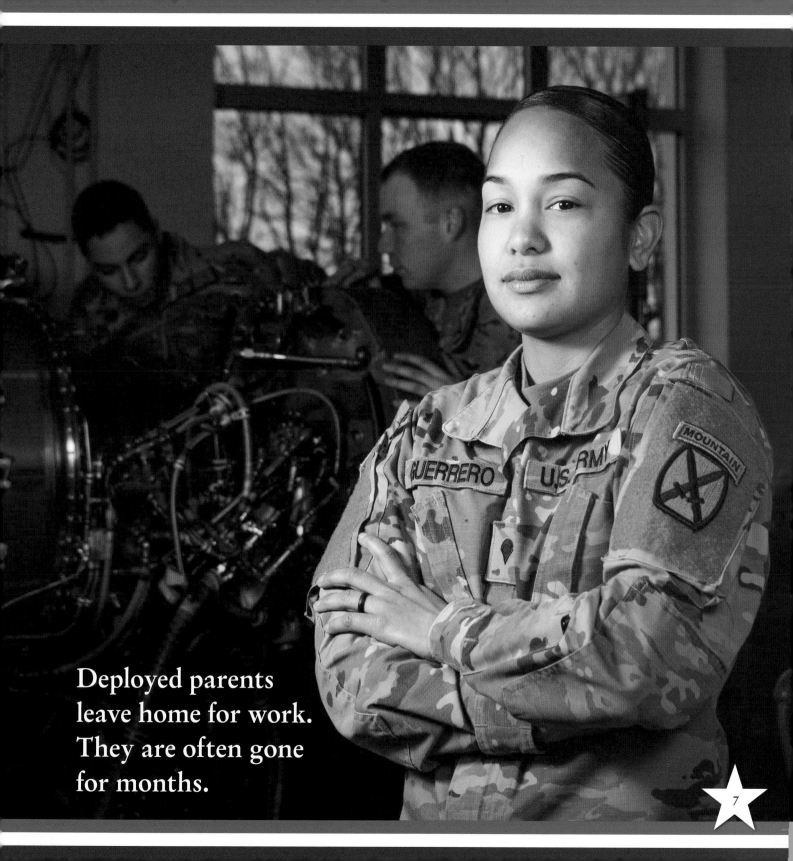

Deployed parents leave home for work. They are often gone for months.

Parents might deploy to another state or a different country.

They can show you on a map where they are going.

On deployment day, you might feel sad and cry. That is okay.

Talking to others about your feelings can help.

When your parent is gone, you miss what you did together. Maybe you miss Mom's bedtime stories or baking with Dad.

Remember that your parent loves you and cares about you.

13

Other loved ones help take care of you.
Grandma teaches you a card game.

A neighbor takes
you to school.

15

You help out at home.
You fold laundry.

You might teach your younger sibling
how to tie shoes or to count.

You keep in touch with your deployed parent.
You write letters or draw pictures to send.

You and your parent can talk on the phone, email, or video chat.

It's normal to feel worried about your mom's or dad's safety.

Remember, deployed parents
are well trained for their jobs.

Each night, draw an *X* on that
day's date on the calendar.

You are one day closer to being reunited.

23

You can plan a homecoming. You might paint a welcome home banner.

With help, you could make
your parent's favorite foods.

For now, you and your parent are apart.

You dream about being together again.

Until then, the love you share keeps your hearts close.

Dear Mom or Dad

You can send a letter and say you love or miss your deployed parent. You might write about everyday things, such as what you are learning in school or how you are helping at home. Tell your parent about special events like your birthday party or school concert. Don't forget to ask how your parent is too.

GLOSSARY

country: a part of the world with its own land and government

deployed: to be moved for military service

military: a country's armed forces

reunited: brought together again

safety: freedom from danger

trained: taught to do something

video chat: a face-to-face talk on the internet

LEARN MORE

Kerley, Barbara. *Brave Like Me.* Washington, DC: National Geographic, 2016.

Military Kids Connect: Feelings
https://militarykidsconnect.health.mil/Feelings

Miller, Marie-Therese. *Parents Like Mine.* Minneapolis: Lerner Publications, 2021.

Redman, Mary. *The Wishing Tree.* Saint Paul: Elva Resa, 2018.

Sesame Street for Military Families: Deployment
https://sesamestreetformilitaryfamilies.org/topic/deployments
/?ytid=X6bK2ayZIBo

INDEX

PHOTO ACKNOWLEDGMENTS

Image credits: Stephanie Santos/1st Armored Division/United States Department of Defense, p. 4; Ohio National Guard photo by Airman 1st Class Christi Richter/flickr (CC BY 2.0), p. 5; Photo by Senior Airman Nichelle Anderson/United States Department of Defense, p. 6; Photo by Sgt. 1st Class Nathan Hutchison/10th Combat Aviation Brigade/United States Department of Defense, p. 7; Air Images/Shutterstock.com, p. 8; realpeople/Shutterstock.com, p. 9; U.S. Air National Guard photo by Master Sgt. Mark C. Olsen/flickr, p. 10; fizkes/Shutterstock.com, p. 11; PR Image Factory/Shutterstock.com, p. 12; michaeljung/Shutterstock.com, p. 13; Phovoir/Shutterstock.com, p. 14; Prasit photo/Moment/Getty Images, p. 15; Ustyle/Shutterstock.com, p. 16; AlohaHawaii/Shutterstock.com, p. 17; Dayna More/Shutterstock.com, p. 18; U.S. Air Force photo by Tech. Sgt. Louis Vega Jr./United States Department of Defense, p. 19; Ann in the uk/Shutterstock.com, p. 20; U.S. Air National Guard photo by Tech. Sgt. Sarah Mattison/flickr (CC BY 2.0), p. 21; Anton Prado PHOTO/Shutterstock.com, p. 22; LightField Studios/Shutterstock.com, p. 23; Erickson Stock/Shutterstock.com, p. 24; bbernard/Shutterstock.com, p. 25; U.S. Marine Corps photo by Cpl. Manuel A. Estrada/United States Department of Defense, p. 26; GalleriaLaureata/Shutterstock.com, p. 27; Prostock-studio/Shutterstock.com, p. 28. Design element: tabosan/Shutterstock.com (camouflage background).

Cover: wavebreakmedia/Shutterstock.com (left); U.S. Navy photo by Mass Communication Specialist 2nd Class Kyle Carlstrom/flickr (CC BY 2.0) (center); New Africa/Shutterstock.com (right).